ALL RI
Origin:

CAUTION: Professionals and amateurs are hereby warned that this play is subject to royalty. It is fully protected by Original Works Publishing, and the copyright laws of the United States. All rights, including professional, amateur, motion pictures, recitation, lecturing, public reading, radio broadcasting, television, and the rights of translation into foreign languages are strictly reserved.

The performance rights to this play are controlled by Original Works Publishing and royalty arrangements and licenses must be secured well in advance of presentation. No changes of any kind shall be made to the work, including without limitation any changes to characterization, intent, time, place, gender or race of the character. PLEASE NOTE that amateur royalty fees are set upon application in accordance with your producing circumstances. When applying for a royalty quotation and license please give us the number of performances intended, dates of production, your seating capacity and admission fee. Royalty of the required amount must be paid whether the play is presented for charity or gain and whether or not admission is charged. Royalties are payable with negotiation from Original Works Publishing.

Due authorship credit must be given anywhere the title appears, on all programs, printing and advertising for the play. The name of the Playwright must appear on a separate line, in which no other name appears, immediately beneath the title and in size and prominence of type equal to 50% of the largest, most prominent letter used for the title of the Work. No person, firm or entity may receive credit larger or more prominent than that accorded to the Playwright.

Copying from this book in whole or in part is strictly forbidden by law, and the right of performance is not transferable. The purchase of this publication does not constitute a license to perform the work.

Whenever the play is produced the following notice must appear on all programs, printing, and advertising for the play on separate line:

"Produced by special arrangement with
Original Works Publishing.
www.originalworksonline.com"

The Water Tribe
© Don Cummings
Trade Edition, 2022
ISBN 978-1-63092-133-0

Also Available From
Original Works Publishing

HEY BROTHER by Bekah Brunstetter
Synopsis: As the saying goes, you can't pick your family. At odds brothers, hard drinking financial planner Ben and grad student Issac, are cohabitating in Ben's beachside North Carolina home and it isn't going well. Adding fuel to their fire is Kris, an Asian-American grad student, who sets her eyes on both of them, forcing a love triangle neither is prepared to handle.
Cast Size: 2 Males, 1 Female

The Water Tribe

by Don Cummings

THE WATER TRIBE had its world premiere January 17, 2020, produced by Ensemble Studio Theatre/Los Angeles in association with VS. Theatre Company. It was directed by Tricia Small. Scenic design and key art were by Adam James Glover. Lighting design was by Shara Abvabi. Costume design was by Michael Mullen. The production stage manager was Maya Braunwarth.

The cast, in order of appearance, was as follows:

Claudia	Hannah Prichard
Johnny	Christopher Reiling
Sydelle	Jayne Taini
Sonia	Alexandra Daniels
Brian	Jon Joseph Gentry

CHARACTERS

CLAUDIA - 20's, smart, good with inputting, clear headed, lower-class white person, great sense of spontaneity with a need to connect. Very present.

JOHNNY - 20's, sincere, confused, wants intimacy, kind, but thrashing underneath it all. Poor. Jewish. Searching hard.

SYDELLE - 60's, secular Jewish woman who does not believe in God, straight forward, pragmatic. Caring. (Pronounced SI-del. Short i.)

BRIAN - Mid-30's, thoughtful, black, serious worker, cautious, alone, scientifically minded.

SONIA - Early-30's. Been through a lot. Has the look of someone who could work for a decorating concern. That is what she does.

THE WATER TRIBE

Scene 1

(Fun night. Studio Apartment. Shabby. On the little table are pizza buns: toasted burger buns with tomato sauce and packaged cheese melted on top. Johnny plays with a knife. A wild animal video plays on the computer. Claudia likes it. Johnny figures out his next move.)

CLAUDIA: You don't need a knife for pizza buns.

(Johnny holds up the knife.)

JOHNNY: It's not for pizza.

CLAUDIA: What's it for?

JOHNNY: These animal videos are boring. Switch back to the last one. I'll show you.

CLAUDIA: Put that down, Johnny. Kiss me.

JOHNNY: Okay.

(They kiss.)

CLAUDIA: Now I'll kiss you.

(Claudia flips Johnny around and gets on top.)

JOHNNY: Ow.

(Johnny switches the video back to the last one.)

JOHNNY: Look. Sometimes they just nick the clitoris. It's not even a full cut.

CLAUDIA: Yeah. And sometimes they remove everything, the labia, all of it, and sew the vagina closed. Look.

JOHNNY: They say these women don't enjoy sex.

CLAUDIA: After that? Who would!

JOHNNY: Before or after.

CLAUDIA: Women enjoy sex. You know that.

(Pause.)

JOHNNY: *(Getting into it.)* The men want power. I want power over you. It's more exciting that way.

CLAUDIA: I want you to have power over me. Sometimes.

JOHNNY: I control you, Claudia.

CLAUDIA: Yeah, right.

JOHNNY: I control you and there is nothing you can do about it.

(Johnny holds up the knife.)

JOHNNY: *(Half-kidding.)* Let me cut out your clit. Just a little.

CLAUDIA: Don't be stupid.

JOHNNY: You like stuff like this.

CLAUDIA: Not right now.

(Claudia pushes Johnny away. Johnny puts down the knife.)

JOHNNY: I did this for you, Claudia. Now what are we going to do?

CLAUDIA: *(Going for the computer.)* The animal videos are better.

JOHNNY: *(Stopping her.)* Nah, let's play Cave War.

CLAUDIA: *(Stopping him.)* That whole game was stolen from Dungeons and Dragons. It's not real. Look at those poor women.

JOHNNY: I am.

CLAUDIA: None of them will ever go to college.

JOHNNY: We didn't go to college.

CLAUDIA: We could have. Maybe. Look at that. That's nuts.

(They watch. Captivated. Awful screaming. Claudia turns down the volume, ready for some fun.)

CLAUDIA: Okay, you nasty man, all sweaty and powerful, I'm ready—Let's pretend you just cut out my clit. Just pretend. And now, it's all over and I can't enjoy sex and I really hate it.

JOHNNY: Great! And I crawl into your cow dung hut and I force myself on you?

CLAUDIA: Sure. It's all about your pleasure.

JOHNNY: You'd like that?

CLAUDIA: If you let me do it to you sometimes.

JOHNNY: I don't know why I want it so much.

CLAUDIA: It's an animal thing.

JOHNNY: To be a man is to be a man.

(Pause.)

CLAUDIA: Yeah? ... Give me that knife.

JOHNNY: Okay.

(Johnny hands Claudia the knife.)

CLAUDIA: Let's see how you like it.

JOHNNY: What are you doing?

CLAUDIA: Let's say we live somewhere where all the male babies get circumcised.

JOHNNY: I'm not circumcised.

CLAUDIA: It's about time then—

JOHNNY: I'm not Jewish.

CLAUDIA: Your mother is.

JOHNNY: Not really.

(Johnny's mother, Sydelle, enters from outside the door with a basket of folded laundry.)

SYDELLE: Look, I'm not one of those self-haters, but I don't believe in religion—

JOHNNY: You told us, Ma—

SYDELLE: Claudia, put down that knife. You'll take someone's eye out.

(Claudia puts down the knife. Johnny changes the video.)

SYDELLE: God, the machines here are so much better than the new place.

JOHNNY: Aren't the machines all new?

SYDELLE: They're cheap. They get clogged. *(To Johnny.)* You have to keep the kitchen clean. You'll get bugs, honey. Remember?

JOHNNY: Bye, Mom.

CLAUDIA: Bye, Sydelle.

(Sydelle leaves.)

JOHNNY: Let's play Cave War.

CLAUDIA: No. Don't change the subject. Your circumcision. Let's begin.

JOHNNY: My father was circumcised. By a rabbi, I bet.

CLAUDIA: How come you're not circumcised?

(Sydelle reenters with an empty bottle of Stain Remover to recycle. Claudia gives up her game.)

SYDELLE: I would never mutilate my child.

CLAUDIA: Isn't it like a ritual you're supposed to have?

SYDELLE: I don't believe in God. And neither should you. Bye, kids.

(Sydelle exits.)

CLAUDIA: Now that she's all moved into the other place, can't she just kind of stay there?

JOHNNY: She doesn't like the machines in her building.

CLAUDIA: They're all brand new.

JOHNNY: Yeah, but they're government issued. They're cheap.

CLAUDIA: Is she lonely? What's going on?

JOHNNY: I don't know.

CLAUDIA: Johnny?

JOHNNY: Yeah?

CLAUDIA: Will you marry me?

JOHNNY: Yeah, sure.

CLAUDIA: But like how we talked about. It would be nice.

JOHNNY: Yeah, I'll ask you.

CLAUDIA: I'll leave Sonia's place. She could come to our wedding. Maybe other people, too.

JOHNNY: It's a good idea.

(Pause.)

CLAUDIA: Yeah, it is. You want to play Cave War? Go ahead.

JOHNNY: Okay.

(Claudia stands up, puts down the knife and straightens out her twisted clothing.)

CLAUDIA: Can I stay over tonight? I don't feel like going back to Sonia's.

JOHNNY: You don't have to ask.

(Johnny plays Cave War on the computer.)

CLAUDIA: Can I have the last pizza bun?

JOHNNY: Sure.

(Claudia pulls out a phone charger and plugs in her old phone.)

CLAUDIA: Who you playing with?

JOHNNY: That guy from Finland.

(Johnny continues to play on his computer. Claudia eats. She watches Johnny.)

CLAUDIA: I bet you win this one.

JOHNNY: You don't ever really win.

CLAUDIA: It just goes on and on?

JOHNNY: Yeah.

CLAUDIA: Don't you ever get tired of it?

JOHNNY: Shhh.

Scene 2

(Claudia and Sonia stand in front of the building where Claudia works. A small cement park. Sonia is Claudia's cousin. She has a lot of good hair. Her coat is almost expensive. Claudia holds a bottle of water with a bow on it.)

SONIA: *(On her phone.)* I'll be there in fifteen minutes ... Yeah, everything's fine. Leaving the doctor's office now ... Need a coffee? ... K.

(Sonia puts her phone away. Claudia hands Sonia a phone charger.)

CLAUDIA: Here.

SONIA: Thanks.

CLAUDIA: Sorry you had to lie. About going to the doctor.

SONIA: I lie to them all the time.

CLAUDIA: You could have stopped at Johnny's. It's closer to your job.

SONIA: Oh, Claudia—

CLAUDIA: We'd love you to visit. You can stop by his place anytime.

SONIA: Yeah. I could.

CLAUDIA: Why do you hate it?

SONIA: I don't hate it.

CLAUDIA: It's been over two years, Sonia. I love him. So—

SONIA: Okay, okay. But Claudia—

CLAUDIA: What?

SONIA: You need to make some other friends. Join a group. Expand your world. Make it real. It can't just be you and Johnny. You might even find someone better.

CLAUDIA: That's a good idea, Sonia. We need some friends.

SONIA: Yeah, you do. Something else. Johnny—

CLAUDIA: I think Johnny would like that.

SONIA: For you, too, Claudia.

CLAUDIA: Just thinking about it makes me calm.

SONIA: Good. And please, don't take my phone charger.

CLAUDIA: I thought it was mine.

SONIA: Okay. But check. I have to go to work. So do you.

CLAUDIA: Don't go yet.

SONIA: I have to.

CLAUDIA: How's your job?

SONIA: Oh, Claudia.

CLAUDIA: So glamorous.

SONIA: You know I hate it.

CLAUDIA: I don't understand.

SONIA: I don't know anything about decorating.

CLAUDIA: You're so stylish.

SONIA: I'd rather work with a bunch of fishermen.

CLAUDIA: You always liked fish.

SONIA: I do. To eat. Maybe more.

CLAUDIA: Or you could be a designer, right?

SONIA: I really need to find something else. We'll see. I have to go.

CLAUDIA: You'll do great anywhere. Look at us, Sonia. We have careers. We did it. Girl power. Right?

SONIA: Yeah, yeah, we did it.

(Sonia twirls the phone charger into her purse and leaves.)

CLAUDIA: When is Carlos moving in with you?

SONIA: I don't … I don't know. It's a mess.

CLAUDIA: Because I totally understand. The situation. That you want the place all to—

SONIA: I really need to go. I have to. Go to work. You're going to be late.

(Claudia watches Sonia leave.)

CLAUDIA: Have a nice day, Sonia!

(Claudia heads off to work.)

Scene 3

(Claudia is at work. She inputs data. She sits alone. She gets up and walks to the next cube. Brian is there. Handsome. Black. He drinks bottled water. He looks up.)

CLAUDIA: Hi.

BRIAN: Yeah?

CLAUDIA: What are you working on?

BRIAN: Bytes per minute for the big guys.

CLAUDIA: I'm still inputting. I don't know if it's for the big guys.

BRIAN: Cool.

(Claudia hands Brian the bottle of water with a ribbon on it.)

BRIAN: What's this?

CLAUDIA: Water.

BRIAN: Why?

CLAUDIA: They were selling them across the street. You always have a bottle going.

BRIAN: Stay hydrated—

CLAUDIA: Yeah, but you go through ten bottles a day or more.

BRIAN: Yeah. I drink a lot.

CLAUDIA: So I got this for you ... Brian?

BRIAN: Yeah?

CLAUDIA: You don't have water where you live?

BRIAN: Partly true.

CLAUDIA: But you live in civilization.

BRIAN: It comes and goes. The water.

CLAUDIA: Okay. Look, I'm just going to cut to it. And it has nothing to do with the water.

BRIAN: What?

CLAUDIA: Do you feel like you're more tribal than white people?

BRIAN: Why?

CLAUDIA: I've never been in a tribe. We were watching videos last night—I'm just wondering.

BRIAN: I have to finish this.

CLAUDIA: Are you more tribal?

BRIAN: Absolutely not.

CLAUDIA: There must be something better about being black—

BRIAN: Why do you think that?

CLAUDIA: I think being black is better. It feels better to me. Like, what people want, how they really are inside. It's more popular.

BRIAN: *(Sarcastic)* Sure.

CLAUDIA: Maybe not.

(Claudia goes back to her cube. There is a long pause while she thinks. She gets back up and walks to Brian.)

CLAUDIA: You ever feel like you're dying or something? Not dying, that's crazy, but like, I remember when I was a little girl, what it was like to look up at all the windows from the street. Or smell a skunk. There were other people out there and I could meet them. Felt good. Smelt good. I'm going to be thirty, one day. My cousin, Sonia, she's older than me. She has more choices. She has a good job, but she's looking around for something else, maybe. I don't know why I'm telling you this.

BRIAN: Is this some pick-up line? Because the black thing was better.

CLAUDIA: No, Brian. It's just—Did you know that little African children—if they're put in a race to win a pile of mangos they all run together so they can tie? They'd rather share the mangos than leave anyone out.

BRIAN: Cool. We should get back to work.

CLAUDIA: I would love that. Be so nice.

BRIAN: I don't know if that's even true, Claudia.

CLAUDIA: Yeah. Maybe people are just lonely. So they share.

BRIAN: Being lonely is the perfect way to repel other people.

CLAUDIA: That's awful.

BRIAN: A paradox.

(Claudia goes back to her cube. They both work.)

CLAUDIA: Hey Brian?

BRIAN: Yeah?

CLAUDIA: I'm almost, officially, getting married. He just has to ask.

BRIAN: To Johnny then?

CLAUDIA: Yeah. We talked about it a bunch of times. Last night, I was pretty straight forward. So—

BRIAN: Sounds like a good plan.

CLAUDIA: You ever going to get married?

BRIAN: I don't know.

CLAUDIA: When you get married, you always have this best friend.

BRIAN: Depends on who you ask.

CLAUDIA: Yeah. But no matter what anyone says, it's true.

(Claudia works. Brian works.)

CLAUDIA: He's fun. And he's sexy. And he doesn't do drugs. He's going to do something with his life.

BRIAN: That's good news. Good for you.

CLAUDIA: He doesn't have a father. He died. But that's okay. What do you want to do?

BRIAN: I'm doing it.

CLAUDIA: 'Cause I thought—you said you liked—

(Claudia notices something sort of awful on her computer screen.)

CLAUDIA: Did you just get an instant message?

BRIAN: From who?

CLAUDIA: My computer is going black in five, four, three, two—Huh.

BRIAN: Sorry.

CLAUDIA: I'm fired.

BRIAN: That's how they do it.

CLAUDIA: Can we still be friends? Are we friends?

BRIAN: Sure. Security is probably coming. Take care of yourself.

(Claudia walks to the door. She sees security coming.)

CLAUDIA: *(Toward the hall.)* Don't worry. I'm on my way out. *(To Brian.)* I'll call you. Bye.

(Claudia leaves.)

(Brian is afraid the same thing is about to happen to him. He waits. It doesn't. Brian continues to work. Relieved.)

Scene 4

(Sydelle stands across from Johnny in his apartment. She takes out round containers of Indian food she brought in.)

SYDELLE: So now neither one of you has a job. Maybe I should move back in, Johnny.

JOHNNY: I'll get one. Why did you name me John? Just John?

SYDELLE: It's simple. And strong.

JOHNNY: But we're Jewish.

SYDELLE: How many times do I have to tell you I don't care about that?

JOHNNY: You're the only Jewish person on earth who doesn't.

SYDELLE: I was born in this country. My parents were born here. My grandparents were born here. And back in the old country, there were no terrible stories. I have nothing to be Jewish about.

JOHNNY: What about Dad?

SYDELLE: Johnny—

JOHNNY: You don't have one picture of him?

SYDELLE: He snapped the photos. Fathers are never in the pictures.

JOHNNY: Sometimes when I look at Claudia, I can imagine what she's going to look like as an old woman.

SYDELLE: Don't do that.

JOHNNY: I can't help it.

SYDELLE: I want you to be happy, Johnny. Claudia, is she really—

JOHNNY: Yeah. She is.

SYDELLE: My son. My delicate son.

JOHNNY: I'm not delicate.

SYDELLE: I just want to make sure you're okay. Okay?

JOHNNY: Okay!

SYDELLE: Okay, okay ... Oh, damn.

JOHNNY: What?

SYDELLE: I ordered three different dishes and they all look like lentils.

JOHNNY: I like lentils.

SYDELLE: Get spoons.

(Johnny gets spoons.)

SYDELLE: Are you depressed?

JOHNNY: No.

SYDELLE: You seem depressed to me. Not clinical, so I'm not too worried. You just need a job, Johnny. You're really smart. That's really all. You can work.

JOHNNY: Of course.

SYDELLE: Life is simple. Right? Claudia seems to know that. Work. Eat. Take care of yourself. Be nice to people. You can make things better for yourself. I know you. You can.

JOHNNY: Okay, mom. Okay.

(The door opens. Claudia enters with a white paper bag of food.)

CLAUDIA: I bought meatball heroes.

SYDELLE: I hope you got one for me.

CLAUDIA: I didn't know—

SYDELLE: I'm joking. It's okay.

(Sydelle covers her food up and packs it away.)

JOHNNY: You don't have to go.

SYDELLE: I can't make you eat these lentils …

(Big pause as they all look at each other. What's next?)

SYDELLE: I'll take them home.

CLAUDIA: Bye, Sydelle.

SYDELLE: … Okay.

JOHNNY: Bye, Mom.

(Sydelle leaves.)

CLAUDIA: Why is she always here?

JOHNNY: She's not.

CLAUDIA: She's here a lot.

(Claudia crawls on top of Johnny and then rolls him over on top of her.)

JOHNNY: Ow.

CLAUDIA: Stop complaining. Come on, take it!

(Claudia tickles Johnny.)

JOHNNY: Ow. Stop. Stop it, Claudia. Stop!

(Johnny pushes Claudia off. She thumps.)

CLAUDIA: Ow.

(Pause.)

CLAUDIA: That didn't even hurt. I was just surprised.

JOHNNY: Let's eat.

CLAUDIA: Okay ...

(Claudia grabs Johnny extra exuberantly.)

JOHNNY: What are you doing?

CLAUDIA: Hugging you.

JOHNNY: That's not fun, Claudia.

(Claudia releases him. She opens the bag of sandwiches and throws one at Johnny.)

JOHNNY: We're adults now, Claudia. Let's, you know, it's time to act like adults.

CLAUDIA: I couldn't agree more. Let's grow up. Make some friends. Take a trip to the mountains.

(Claudia takes a bite of her sandwich.)

JOHNNY: Sorry about your job.

CLAUDIA: It only took me nine months to find that one. So, you know—

(Pause.)

JOHNNY: Will you marry me?

CLAUDIA: Johnny?

JOHNNY: This work thing. You must feel awful.

CLAUDIA: This is the big romantic night? You're really asking?

JOHNNY: Yeah, I want to marry you. Let's—I'm asking you—Officially.

CLAUDIA: So like, when I'm down, that's when you want to marry me?

JOHNNY: I don't want to marry you because you're down.

CLAUDIA: Fuck!

(Claudia punches her sandwich and makes a mess.)

CLAUDIA: Fuck, fuck!

JOHNNY: What's wrong with you?

(Claudia leaves to get something to clean up the mess. Johnny sits there looking at the mess. Claudia returns.)

CLAUDIA: Here's the thing. Something's wrong. We've been together for almost three years and we never go out.

JOHNNY: We don't have any money.

CLAUDIA: But we need friends, Johnny. Like a group, right? Or some, I don't know—something bigger than watching videos and playing Cave War. Your mother always around. Something, like—something! It'll be good for us.

JOHNNY: I'm not enough?

CLAUDIA: You are! But, we need, we need friends. Like be in some sort of tribe. One that wants to change the world for the better. We could be part of it.

JOHNNY: Religion makes people happy.

(Claudia looks at her meatball hero. She picks it up and she holds it.)

CLAUDIA: I don't understand religion.

JOHNNY: Okay. I hear you. I found you a new one today.

CLAUDIA: What?

JOHNNY: A lion eating a baby zebra.

CLAUDIA: We've seen that one before.

JOHNNY: Not this one. A zebra gives birth and within just ten seconds, a lion jumps the baby zebra and eats it.

CLAUDIA: Turn it on.

JOHNNY: Okay.

(Claudia and Johnny sit on the couch and watch the computer while they eat their meatball heroes. They are returned to their most natural state. They both take bites of their sandwiches and keep watching.)

CLAUDIA: I love you Johnny.

JOHNNY: I love you, Claudia.

(This video gets them hot. They put down their sandwiches. They start making out. It gets wild and heated. There's a lump under the cushion. It's the Bible. Claudia pulls it out from under the cushion and tosses it across the room.)

JOHNNY: Hey.

CLAUDIA: Bite me.

JOHNNY: Okay.

(Johnny bites her on the arm.)

CLAUDIA: That feels good ... I'll talk to Sonia. And my friend Brian, first.

JOHNNY: What for?

CLAUDIA: Dates and stuff. For our wedding. Make a plan. We'll have people there—

JOHNNY: Okay.

(Claudia stares at Johnny.)

JOHNNY: Come here.

(Claudia takes off her shirt. She bites Johnny once.)

JOHNNY: Ow ...

(Johnny flips Claudia over and pins her.)

CLAUDIA: You're a monster!

JOHNNY: My father was a monster.

(The computer screen catches Claudia's eye.)

CLAUDIA: Wait! Wait!

JOHNNY: What?

CLAUDIA: *(Off the computer.)* Look at that baby zebra.

JOHNNY: Chewed in half.

CLAUDIA: Never even had a chance.

(Johnny takes off his shirt. He looks down at her.)

CLAUDIA: Okay. Now.

JOHNNY: *(Going for it.)* That's right.

CLAUDIA: Yeah, Johnny … Yeah, I'll marry you.

Scene 5

(Evening. Claudia and Brian both arrive at the same time in front of the building where Claudia used to work. The small cement park. Brian from inside the building. Claudia from one side. Claudia holds a bottle of water with a ribbon on it, hands it to Brian.)

CLAUDIA: I got you another one.

BRIAN: Funny.

(Shadows of people walk by.)

CLAUDIA: I like this park.

BRIAN: They have to build a certain amount of public space … They didn't replace you. Upstairs. Budget cuts. There's not much work.

(Pause.)

CLAUDIA: So you're in that room all alone?

BRIAN: Yeah.

CLAUDIA: Must be awful.

BRIAN: I don't mind.

CLAUDIA: Brian ... Are we friends?

BRIAN: I think so.

CLAUDIA: But I mean, like, real friends.

BRIAN: Depends on what you mean.

CLAUDIA: I don't know. I'm not so good at this. My parents died.

BRIAN: I didn't know that.

CLAUDIA: I mean, they died when I was young. When I was, well, actually—

BRIAN: It's okay.

CLAUDIA: My dad died when I was twelve. My mom, she's still alive. Somewhere. But really, it's like she's dead because, well, it's like she's dead.

BRIAN: I still see my mom. My dad took off.

CLAUDIA: Sorry.

BRIAN: People have a hard time staying together.

CLAUDIA: It's tough.

BRIAN: It is. So I keep myself on the straight and narrow.

CLAUDIA: Yeah, but—

BRIAN: There's not a lot of room …

CLAUDIA: So what's the deal with your water situation?

BRIAN: You can't drink it in our neighborhood. There are problems. Pipes.

CLAUDIA: Sorry … Can we be friends?

BRIAN: We are Claudia.

CLAUDIA: I don't really know you. I know you don't have a father—now. You watch science shows, you said—what else do you like?

BRIAN: I like to get a paycheck. I watch some TV. I like to read about how the world works. Geology. Plants and animals. I like philosophy. Honestly, there's not much to know.

CLAUDIA: You're nice. I always wonder, like, can someone be nice but still be exciting? And I think you might be that way. Kind of nice and exciting. Full of possibility.

BRIAN: Claudia, I feel like you're coming on to me. And it confuses me because you're going to marry this guy.

CLAUDIA: Yeah, it's official.

BRIAN: Then what's going on?

CLAUDIA: I'm not coming on to you Brian. I just— *(Truly vulnerable.)* I just want to know if you'll be my friend.

(Brian puts his hand on Claudia's shoulder.)

BRIAN: Sure.

CLAUDIA: Thank you. I don't really trust women.

BRIAN: They can be tricky.

CLAUDIA: My mom—

BRIAN: I understand.

CLAUDIA: My cousin, Sonia, she's my family I guess, but not a friend. She says we need friends.

BRIAN: So we'll be friends then.

CLAUDIA: But not like American friends. Because American friends are, well, everyone drinks and runs around, and they post it online.

BRIAN: But we're Americans.

CLAUDIA: I was thinking we'd be more like in a tribe with a few other people. That's why I'm asking—

BRIAN: I'm not much of a joiner.

CLAUDIA: Everything will be built in. We could do things, you know, that help each other.

BRIAN: I don't think I need help—

CLAUDIA: Everyone needs help. Like, Johnny and I could bring you water. We could make sure you always had clean water to drink. How's that?

BRIAN: You don't have to do that.

CLAUDIA: Johnny, he's really reliable. You could always count on him.

BRIAN: Yeah, but I can just go to the store and buy water. The big box store sells water.

CLAUDIA: But someone else could do it for you sometimes. And you could do something for them. You know, make a meal. Or patrol the area. We could do things—together.

BRIAN: Sure.

CLAUDIA: You have a girlfriend? She could be part of our tribe, too, you know?

BRIAN: No I don't.

CLAUDIA: Are you gay?

BRIAN: My girlfriend broke up with me.

CLAUDIA: Sorry.

BRIAN: She ran off with a doctor.

CLAUDIA: Sorry.

BRIAN: It's okay. He was a smart guy. Further along than me.

CLAUDIA: Listen—you're going to meet Johnny. We'll have you over for dinner or we'll have some lunch, first and then have you over for dinner. We'll do good things.

BRIAN: Okay.

CLAUDIA: That's great.

BRIAN: Great ... You sure you aren't all twisted and fucked up and just trying to get into my pants, Claudia?

CLAUDIA: I'm not. No.

BRIAN: 'Cause let me tell you something. I think you're probably a good person. But I also think you're a little crazy.

CLAUDIA: Really?

BRIAN: But I can't tell what kind of crazy you are and I have seen some crazy in my life. So I think maybe you aren't crazy yet but maybe you will be crazy in the future and this is what crazy looks like before it hits thirty. You want me to be friends with you and this phantom Johnny and all I can think is maybe you both want to get in my pants. Is that what's going on here, Claudia? Because people do some weird shit and I need to go back to school and get a real degree—

CLAUDIA: Okay—

BRIAN: —and I need some more money so I have to keep things on the straight and narrow.

CLAUDIA: You have a cool imagination. Thank you for being so honest. But Johnny and I don't want that, Brian. I think our tribe could be a tribe of people who are honest, all the time.

BRIAN: So this isn't about sex?

CLAUDIA: I want you to meet Johnny.

BRIAN: Okay.

CLAUDIA: And as a friend, you could let me know what you think of him. And if you like him, you can join our tribe.

BRIAN: Okay. Sorry.

CLAUDIA: We could meet you for lunch? We could meet you here.

BRIAN: Okay.

(Claudia gets real close.)

CLAUDIA: No one has any friends anymore.

(Claudia's phone makes a sound. She looks.)

CLAUDIA: I got a job!

BRIAN: Great, Claudia. What is it?

(Brian goes to hug her in congratulations. In her excitement Claudia misses his approach.)

CLAUDIA: Marketing. I'm so glad we're friends. I can't wait to tell Johnny. Okay?

BRIAN: Sure.

CLAUDIA: Thank you Brian. Thanks for seeing me. Bye.

(Claudia shakes Brian's hand and runs off.)

Scene 6

(Sydelle wears a thirty-year old wedding gown. Johnny tries to zip it up the back.)

SYDELLE: This is stupid. I'm too fat.

JOHNNY: No you're not. Wait.

SYDELLE: You're gonna rip it.

JOHNNY: No I won't.

SYDELLE: Thirty-two years ago. I was just a girl. I was tiny. *(She twirls.)* Get me out of this thing. I don't want to do this.

JOHNNY: What did Dad wear?

SYDELLE: A blue suit. Stop it, Johnny. This isn't—

JOHNNY: Were you married by a rabbi?

SYDELLE: It was quick. Don't get married Johnny.

JOHNNY: And there're no pictures?

CLAUDIA: *(Unseen, coming up the apartment stairs.)* Johnny!

JOHNNY: Oh my God.

SYDELLE: Oh my God. Get this off me.

JOHNNY: It's too late!

SYDELLE: Get it off. This was an awful idea, John!

(Johnny works on the zipper.)

JOHNNY: It's stuck.

SYDELLE: What?

(Claudia works the lock outside the door.)

JOHNNY: It won't go up or down. Maybe you should hide.

SYDELLE: She'll be here all night.

JOHNNY: I don't know what to tell you.

(The Door. Claudia enters.)

CLAUDIA: I got a job.

SYDELLE: That's great.

CLAUDIA: *(To Johnny.)* I think you should apply, too, Johnny! Everything's working out!

SYDELLE: That's wonderful Claudia.

CLAUDIA: *(To Sydelle.)* What are you doing in that dress?

SYDELLE: This smelly old thing?

JOHNNY: It's stuck.

CLAUDIA: Why are you wearing that?

SYDELLE: I found it during the move—

CLAUDIA: Why do you have it on?

SYDELLE: Johnny?

JOHNNY: 'Cause—I thought—

CLAUDIA: *(To Sydelle.)* Did Johnny tell you we were getting married? We didn't announce—

SYDELLE: I'm sorry. Johnny?

(Sydelle turns her back to Claudia. The dress is bulging.)

SYDELLE: Just rip it off me. It's stuck. The zipper is broken. Just rip it.

(Claudia rips it.)

SYDELLE: Thank you.

(Sydelle goes into the kitchen to put on regular clothes.)

CLAUDIA: Sydelle, is that your old wedding dress?

SYDELLE: *(From kitchen.)* God, I'm sorry—

CLAUDIA: *(To Johnny.)* What are you doing?

JOHNNY: You didn't tell me not to tell her.

CLAUDIA: Who else did you tell?

JOHNNY: The Finnish guy I play Cave War with—why is this such a big deal?

(Sydelle, dressed, enters with the wedding dress balled up. She leaves it.)

SYDELLE: Have a good night. I'm, I'm going.

CLAUDIA: *(To Johnny.)* The Finnish guy? He's a stranger.

SYDELLE: *(To Johnny.)* I told you this was a terrible idea.

JOHNNY: We've been playing Cave War for a long time. He's my friend.

CLAUDIA: He's not a friend! He lives in Finland!

SYDELLE: *(To Claudia.)* It is his friend.

CLAUDIA: That's not a friend! Sydelle, I respect you because you're going to be my mother-in-law. And I think you're maybe kind of lonely—

(Pause.)

SYDELLE: Mm-Hm.

CLAUDIA: And we want you in our lives ...

SYDELLE: ... Mm-Hm.

CLAUDIA: But you're here all the time ... Johnny?

SYDELLE: He thought maybe you would like my dress. We thought you would be home later. That's all. It was a mistake.

CLAUDIA: We're just going downtown.

SYDELLE: I don't know if it's a good idea—

CLAUDIA: You'll join us. You'll be a witness, then. Okay?

SYDELLE: I mean—the wedding.

JOHNNY: It's a good idea.

SYDELLE: *(To Johnny.)* You can't take care of yourself. You were arrested for stealing.

CLAUDIA: He was arrested for being a vagrant.

SYDELLE: You were living in someone's car!

CLAUDIA: He was traveling.

SYDELLE: He was homeless!

CLAUDIA: He's not homeless now!

SYDELLE: Because I gave him this apartment!

JOHNNY: That was two years ago! I was just in jail one night. And it wasn't even hardcore. You have to stop worrying, Mom. I can take care of myself.

CLAUDIA: We can, Sydelle.

SYDELLE: Okay, listen to me. I didn't have good luck with being married so maybe I don't know anything, but you're young, you're both unemployed—

CLAUDIA: I got a job!

SYDELLE: A temporary job?

CLAUDIA: So what?

SYDELLE: Just—whatever you do—Don't have children.

(Sydelle exits.)

CLAUDIA: She's here all the time.

JOHNNY: I—

CLAUDIA: And it's weird. And now I have a job, so I bet you don't want to marry me anymore.

JOHNNY: Why not?

CLAUDIA: Because when I'm down, you get in the mood. But when things go my way—

JOHNNY: You know what, Claudia? That's just not fucking true.

CLAUDIA: What?

JOHNNY: You go up and down so much—

CLAUDIA: That's just normal.

JOHNNY: —it's like random numbers being spit out in a computer program. I'm just being me, Claudia, and you, you try to tell me what I am based on this wild ride you're living?

CLAUDIA: Your ride is wild, too, Johnny! You go up and down. You waste time playing Cave War. You play dress-up with your mother. She bugs me. I don't know why. But now I do. You tell me I can stay over but I can tell you just want me to go back to Sonia's so you can play games.

JOHNNY: That's just normal! I don't do what I do because you have a job or you don't have a job. Or you're up or you're down or whatever the hell is going on. It's not weird to have my mother visit us.

CLAUDIA: You don't know what you're doing.

JOHNNY: Oh, eat my pussy.

CLAUDIA: Eat MY pussy!

JOHNNY: No, you eat MY pussy.

CLAUDIA: I'll eat your fucking pussy.

(Claudia jumps on top of Johnny and knocks him onto the couch.)

JOHNNY: Yeah?

CLAUDIA: Yeah.

JOHNNY: Yeah, baby?

CLAUDIA: Yeah. So who's gonna eat whose pussy?

(A long pause. Claudia really looks at Johnny—taking him in.)

CLAUDIA: We're good together.

JOHNNY: Yeah. We are.

(A long pause. Claudia really stares at Johnny. Then, Claudia sits up and she pulls Johnny toward her.)

JOHNNY: What are you doing?

CLAUDIA: Shh.

(Claudia pulls Johnny harder, down into her lap.)

JOHNNY: Claudia?

(Johnny lies in Claudia's lap. She strokes his hair.)

CLAUDIA: I'm going to take care of you.

JOHNNY: I don't need—

CLAUDIA: Yeah you do. We both do. We'll prove your mother wrong.

JOHNNY: Sorry. It really was my idea. I thought maybe you'd like her old dress.

CLAUDIA: It smells. It's yellow. And now it's ripped. Crazy idea.

JOHNNY: She has the dress, but no pictures.

CLAUDIA: I told someone, too. I hope that's okay.

JOHNNY: Who?

CLAUDIA: Brian. From my old job.

JOHNNY: That's okay.

CLAUDIA: But only because I want you to meet him.

JOHNNY: Okay.

CLAUDIA: Now I'm going to take care of you.

JOHNNY: I'll take care of you, too.

(Claudia continues to stroke Johnny's hair. He turns around and starts unbuttoning her pants.)

JOHNNY: What's your job?

CLAUDIA: It's in marketing.

JOHNNY: That's a good job. I'll get a job, too.

CLAUDIA: I know you will. We're gonna be fine. And we're going to get married. Let's fuck.

(They get ready to fuck.)

Scene 7

(Next morning, Sonia stands in the middle of the room checking her phone. The Bible is on the table. Sonia stares at the distasteful apartment. Claudia enters from the kitchen side with two cups of coffee.)

CLAUDIA: I got a new job.

SONIA: When do you start?

CLAUDIA: Right after the weekend. It's in marketing.

SONIA: Great. What is it?

CLAUDIA: I'm going to be a Liker. Thanks for coming over.

SONIA: What's that?

CLAUDIA: It's an internet thing Sonia. It's not a big job. But I think it's going to last a while. And I get to work from home.

SONIA: Good.

CLAUDIA: So, I wanted to ask you—

SONIA: Where's Johnny?

CLAUDIA: He had to have one of those unemployment meetings to prove he's unemployed.

SONIA: Okay. Thanks for the coffee, Claudia, listen, I came over because I need to tell you something.

CLAUDIA: I need to tell you something, too.

SONIA: But this is pretty important so I had to tell you in person.

CLAUDIA: So, Sonia, get ready—

SONIA: It's not great news—

CLAUDIA: Just hold on. Listen. I'm getting married.

SONIA: Claudia?

CLAUDIA: To Johnny. We're getting married.

SONIA: Oh, Claudia.

CLAUDIA: He's looking for a job, Sonia. He wants to be something, really. And we have fun together. We love each other.

SONIA: Johnny's nice ... I can't pay for it, Claudia.

CLAUDIA: No, no, that's not it.

SONIA: Don't do it, Claudia. It's—it's impulsive. And, why don't you get a degree instead? In anything. Nursing.

CLAUDIA: I don't want to be a nurse. I'm good with computers and organizing. I don't have money for school.

SONIA: You could be head nurse. You could run a department. More sugar?

CLAUDIA: I'll get it. So this is the question, ready?

SONIA: Sure. But—

CLAUDIA: Will you be my maid of honor? Be in the wedding pictures? Be in our group?

SONIA: How are you going to afford it?

CLAUDIA: It only costs sixty bucks at the courthouse. And then we're going to have a nice dinner. Johnny's mother will pay for it. Something—You like French food?

SONIA: Yeah—

CLAUDIA: Great. And you can bring your fancy boyfriend.

SONIA: Claudia, I don't even know if—

CLAUDIA: We're building a tribe, Sonia. Witnesses. Your idea. And we'll all know each other forever. You're my family and Johnny has his mother—she's around too much, but I don't hate her, well, I hate her a little, but I think that's normal—and then there's this guy Brian from work.

SONIA: But you work from home—

CLAUDIA: He's from my old job. He's really nice. You can bring Carlos. Then there'd be like six of us. You said I should have more people around—

SONIA: When is it, Claudia?

CLAUDIA: Well, I thought I'd ask you when is good for you? You'll bring Carlos?

SONIA: Sure, I can bring Carlos. If we're still together.

CLAUDIA: What?

SONIA: The noise. He's loud. I don't know.

CLAUDIA: But you're still a couple, right?

SONIA: Claudia—It's all falling apart. You can't, I can't—Don't use me as your role model. Listen—

CLAUDIA: It's not about that—

SONIA: I just think—I need to leave this town. Give it all up. I'm hanging on by a thread here.

CLAUDIA: You have your great job.

SONIA: I hate my job. They're all experts. They all know what's beautiful. They have art history degrees. Some went to business school. I feel like an idiot.

CLAUDIA: You're so beautiful, Sonia. You fit right in. So when are you free?

SONIA: Well, there's the foundation meeting next week. And then—

CLAUDIA: No, this summer. Let's do it over the summer.

SONIA: I have a trip. I'm going to Milan with my boss for a week in July. I don't know which one yet. And there's the big fundraiser for the autism thing. She has not one, but two kids with autism. Then Carlos wants to go to Puerto Rico for a week to see his mother. I don't want to go. I really don't.

CLAUDIA: Well, how about August for the wedding?

SONIA: Yeah, maybe late August—I might be free the second half of August.

CLAUDIA: Okay good. I can plan it for then. Like August twenty-something. Would that work?

SONIA: Sure, sure, Claudia.

CLAUDIA: 'Cause I want you to be my maid of honor. And we'll all go out as a group. To celebrate. You probably should meet everyone first. I can have everyone over for dinner.

SONIA: I understand.

(Pause.)

SONIA: Your life has no context, Claudia.

CLAUDIA: What do you mean?

SONIA: This room—Like at work, we always refer to something—we ground our stuff in an environment people know and understand. A Provençal summer evening, international hotel chic, the faded romance of the Etruscans.

CLAUDIA: Is that how a design site works? What are Etruscans?

SONIA: They were absorbed by the Romans, they tell me. People need a point of reference. Our site caters to people who have done well. They own a boat, or they have three houses. We know what their world is and we know what defines that world and we service it, in context.

CLAUDIA: How did you learn all that?

SONIA: I didn't. I don't really know the exact style of anything. My boss, she does. She knows everything. She studied it.

CLAUDIA: How did you get this job?

SONIA: My boss likes to have assistants that look like her. I've been told. But she doesn't like them to be a threat.

CLAUDIA: That's crazy, Sonia.

SONIA: Yeah, but that's something else. You need context. This place, this room, this—

CLAUDIA: Is context about money? I need a permanent job. I'd love to do what you do.

SONIA: No you wouldn't. It wouldn't suit you. You need to do something more grounded. More practical. Like a skill. Bus driver. Dental records. You need context.

You need a world to understand, Claudia. This room. This—are you going to live in this room with Johnny after you get married?

CLAUDIA: Yeah.

SONIA: And this is going to be your world? This room?

CLAUDIA: People in Africa have it worse. People in Asia live in boxes. This is going to be great.

SONIA: No it isn't.

CLAUDIA: Sure it is.

SONIA: It's nowhere, Claudia. You live—this is nowhere. And I'm not being a bitch here. Just, you need something more defined. Something real. Even our little place in high school was better than this.

CLAUDIA: Your mother—

SONIA: Yeah. She did the best she could. Gone forever. Claudia—

CLAUDIA: Don't be so sad, Sonia. Come to dinner one night to meet everyone before the wedding. I want you to meet Johnny's mother. We can all sit down with our calendars.

SONIA: I've met his mother.

CLAUDIA: But really meet her. And Brian from my old job. Carlos. It'll be fun.

SONIA: Okay. Sure.

CLAUDIA: Thanks, Sonia.

SONIA: Okay, I heard your plan. Now listen to me—

(Sonia hands Claudia a small piece of paper.)

CLAUDIA: What's this?

SONIA: Your mother is dying.

CLAUDIA: Again?

SONIA: She gave my phone number to the hospital. I'm sorry.

CLAUDIA: I don't want to see her.

SONIA: She's dying. She has liver failure.

CLAUDIA: Nothing can kill her.

SONIA: Maybe not. Who knows. But it's liver failure. I have to go to work. Face all the beauty.

(Sonia leaves the paper on a table.)

CLAUDIA: I hope Carlos can come to dinner. Help us pick a date. Meet everyone. Is he moving in with you? I thought you wanted me to move out for Carlos—

SONIA: I don't know. I really don't. But I've got to do something, Claudia. Maybe do the fishing thing in North Carolina. I was interviewed. Maybe move in with Carlos. Maybe he'll come with me. Or something else. So—that's how it is.

CLAUDIA: Okay …

SONIA: *(Emphatic, with finality.)* … Moving out of my place is no fucking reason to get married. You're feral, Claudia, you know what that means?

CLAUDIA: Yeah, like a cat.

SONIA: Like a cat without a home. Your mother was useless. But that's over. You're smart. You don't have to marry someone just because you need a place to live.

CLAUDIA: I know that. I love Johnny.

SONIA: But Claudia ... No job. The wild animal videos. Cave War—

CLAUDIA: We have fun. We have good sex.

SONIA: You just keep biting each other. Like wild animals.

CLAUDIA: I do most of the biting. He wants to be a better man than his father. Or he wants to be like him. He was Jewish—

SONIA: Great. But honey, Johnny's not Jewish or anything, really, he's like, he's, Claudia, he's—

CLAUDIA: What?

SONIA: He's, he's nothing.

CLAUDIA: Maybe I'm nothing then, too, okay? I'm going to marry him and we're going to have a great group of friends. And we'll be something. We'll form some kind of tribe. We'll make our own context. We'll be like Etruscans—or Jewish. But I don't get religion. I don't know. Something.

SONIA: Keep trying, Claudia. It's your time. I have to go to my miserable fucking job. Go see your mother.

CLAUDIA: Is she really dying?

SONIA: Possibly.

CLAUDIA: I'll never find her. It's never worth it.

(Sonia pushes the piece of paper toward Claudia.)

SONIA: Start here. Then hit the other places ... You latch onto things, that's what you do. You should maybe latch onto something else is what I'm saying. I have to go.

(Sonia leaves. Claudia picks up the piece of paper and looks at it. She puts on her shoes.)

Scene 8

(Midday. Park outside Claudia's old job. Claudia wheels a large red cart of bottled water. Johnny follows her. They're nervous about meeting Brian.)

JOHNNY: You're rubbing.

(They stop. Claudia kicks the lowest flat of bottles away from the wheels.)

CLAUDIA: He's never late.

JOHNNY: What does he like to do?

CLAUDIA: He's a good guy. Like a family guy.

JOHNNY: A family guy is married. He's not married.

CLAUDIA: No, but he's got brothers and sisters and a mother. He's nice. You'll like him. You might become best friends.

JOHNNY: Okay.

(Brian arrives.)

BRIAN: Sorry I'm late. I had to do some extra—

CLAUDIA: Hi.

BRIAN: Hi Claudia. Johnny?

JOHNNY: Yeah. Hello Brian.

(Brian and Johnny shake hands.)

BRIAN: Pleasure to meet you.

JOHNNY: You, too.

BRIAN: Claudia says you're getting married.

JOHNNY: We are. It's …

BRIAN: … Where do you want to eat? *(To Claudia.)* You like that Japanese place.

JOHNNY: We don't like Japanese food. I can eat a sandwich or something.

(Claudia wheels the cart a second.)

CLAUDIA: Um— *(To Brian.)* These are for you.

BRIAN: Claudia?

CLAUDIA: I know you can get your own. But let's say it's your birthday and someone bought you a gift, you have to take it, right?

BRIAN: Right.

CLAUDIA: It's a little weird.

JOHNNY: I told her it was a little weird.

BRIAN: No, it's fine. They won't go to waste.

CLAUDIA: I knew you'd need something to wheel them home. I thought about that—But maybe it's big and inconvenient?

BRIAN: You got caught up—

CLAUDIA: Yeah.

JOHNNY: She was all excited. We were horsing around the aisles and we were looking at the paper towel holders. We're thinking of getting one because when you leave a roll on the counter, a lot of times the towels get wet. And that's not fun, so—

CLAUDIA: And I said to Johnny—We should buy something for Brian.

JOHNNY: And I thought that was a great idea. We like buying things for people.

CLAUDIA: We usually don't have a lot of money.

JOHNNY: Well, sometimes we do. Sometimes we have money.

CLAUDIA: I start my job tomorrow.

BRIAN: Where is it? We could have lunch more—

CLAUDIA: Well, I do it from home. It's an internet job, the marketing job. So we were in the store—

JOHNNY: And I was in the paper towel aisle when Claudia rolls up with this cart full of water.

CLAUDIA: Johnny hates these carts.

JOHNNY: They're too big! They take up your whole closet. They're like salad spinners—FWUMP!

CLAUDIA: But I said—Johnny, let's get something for Brian. So, the cart and the water are for you.

BRIAN: You two are like a comedy team.

CLAUDIA: Johnny's the funny one. He's like a comedian and he shoplifts.

JOHNNY: I didn't shoplift.

CLAUDIA: You pretended to. He held up a toilet brush—opened his coat and held it to his chest, like he loved it. But—did he love it or was he stealing it? People looked at him, laughing.

JOHNNY: Then a guard started following us around.

CLAUDIA: He didn't care—

JOHNNY: I put the toilet brush back.

CLAUDIA: But we still should buy a paper towel holder.

JOHNNY: I'll get you that instead of an engagement ring. More useful. *(To Brian.)* You ever been engaged?

BRIAN: No. Close. My girlfriend ran off.

JOHNNY: That does not compute!

BRIAN: The guy was a doctor.

JOHNNY: So what.

BRIAN: He was a specialist. My mother worked with him.

CLAUDIA: What does your mother do?

BRIAN: Office work. For the doctor. That's how my ex met him.

JOHNNY: Nuts!

BRIAN: It wasn't fun.

JOHNNY: That's just bullshit. She didn't deserve you.

CLAUDIA: You should prank her. Call her number and tell her she owes money for taxes or something.

JOHNNY: That never works. We should eat.

CLAUDIA: Yeah, I'm starving.

JOHNNY: I'll eat Japanese. They have chicken?

BRIAN: Sure. Bento Box.

JOHNNY: *(To Brian.)* Bento Box? Okay. You ever play Cave War?

BRIAN: Is that like Dungeons and Dragons?

JOHNNY: *(To Brian.)* A little. I don't have a father either.

CLAUDIA: Johnny!

BRIAN: Mine ran off.

JOHNNY: Mine died. Let's eat!

CLAUDIA: After lunch, I have to go visit my mother.

JOHNNY: I'll come with you.

CLAUDIA: No, I'll do it myself. *(To Brian.)* My mother's dying.

BRIAN: Oh—I'm sorry—

CLAUDIA: Yeah, yeah, it's nothing, because she's always been kind of dead. I grew up with Sonia, and her mother, but mostly Sonia. My aunt, before she got cancer, she was always traveling, with men or whatever, anyway—We should eat lunch first.

BRIAN: You sure?

CLAUDIA: Oh, yeah. She never really dies. And then we'll have you over for dinner soon, too. Like, Friday!

JOHNNY: Well, like, with other people. There'll be other people there.

(They roll off.)

Scene 9

(Johnny and Claudia enter with the cart of water. Johnny also has a bag of canned tomatoes.)

CLAUDIA: It will be easier for him to get the water when he comes to dinner Friday.

JOHNNY: Yeah, but it wasn't easier for us.

CLAUDIA: Put the tomatoes in the kitchen.

JOHNNY: I know ... How could they lose her?

CLAUDIA: She disappears. That's what she does.

JOHNNY: Maybe she'll show up at one of the other hospitals?

CLAUDIA: What a waste of time. I don't have a mother. I never did, really.

JOHN: Even when you were little?

CLAUDIA: I don't remember her being there.

JOHNNY: I hate her.

CLAUDIA: There's not much to hate. Johnny.

JOHNNY: Don't worry about your mom.

(Johnny hugs Claudia.)

CLAUDIA: Thank you for searching with me. Never again.

JOHNNY: Of course.

CLAUDIA: I just have to shake it off. I'm going to do some work.

JOHNNY: I thought you were starting tomorrow.

CLAUDIA: I got my log-in info. No time like the present. So, what are you going to do?

JOHNNY: I could help you. I could help you do the clicking.

(Claudia jumps on Johnny and throws him down to the couch.)

JOHNNY: Ow.

CLAUDIA: You're so nice to me.

(They make out, but Johnny is annoyed about being knocked over.)

JOHNNY: I love you, Claudia, but—

CLAUDIA: I love you, Johnny.

JOHNNY: You're really beautiful, and—

CLAUDIA: I'm really not. I'm kind of sexy but I'm not a regular beauty.

JOHNNY: I would hate that. You're more beautiful than that. You're alive, Claudia.

CLAUDIA: We both are.

(Claudia bites Johnny.)

JOHNNY: But stop biting me!

CLAUDIA: Okay, bite me. Bite my arm.

JOHNNY: Nah.

CLAUDIA: Just do it.

JOHNNY: I don't want to bite you. And I don't want you to bite me.

CLAUDIA: You like it when I bite you.

JOHNNY: It's embarrassing.

CLAUDIA: No it isn't.

JOHNNY: Kind of—

CLAUDIA: Really? It's just fun. Bite me.

JOHNNY: I feel trapped.

CLAUDIA: Bite me.

JOHNNY: On a bridge or I don't know.

CLAUDIA: Just bite me, Johnny. It's no big deal.

JOHNNY: Okay.

(Johnny bites her arm.)

CLAUDIA: Harder.

(Johnny bites her harder.)

CLAUDIA: Yeah, good. Bite my ass.

(Johnny bites her ass.)

CLAUDIA: HARDER!

(Johnny bites harder.)

CLAUDIA: My big toe just went numb … Okay! Stop! I've got stuff to do.

(Claudia pushes him off. Johnny is very put off by all of this.)

CLAUDIA: I'm going to work for an hour. I just have to like things. Sometimes write a comment.

JOHNNY: Okay.

CLAUDIA: This is important. Okay? I want to start working. Get a jump on things. It's easy stuff.

(Claudia gets a snack and a few things ready to work.)

JOHNNY: I think Brian likes you.

CLAUDIA: He likes both of us. He's nice, right?

JOHNNY: He understands String Theory. Seems like—

CLAUDIA: I never heard of it before.

JOHNNY: It looked like you did. I heard of it once. Is he going to be a scientist?

CLAUDIA: I don't know. We could all live on the moon together. Wouldn't that be fun? ... All right, I'm going to work for a couple hours and later we'll eat and fuck. Okay? ... What?

JOHNNY: I think I got a job, Claudia.

CLAUDIA: Where?

JOHNNY: So now we'll both be working.

CLAUDIA: What's the job?

JOHNNY: Janitor.

CLAUDIA: Really? That's—Where?

JOHNNY: At the temple on Fourteenth.

CLAUDIA: When did you apply?

JOHNNY: After I went to my unemployment meeting.

CLAUDIA: Why didn't you tell me?

JOHNNY: I don't have it yet. I don't want to jinx it. The rabbi was nice.

CLAUDIA: When will you know?

JOHNNY: Soon. Nice guy. The rabbi. He has some ideas. We've been talking. He didn't know my father.

CLAUDIA: Why would he?

JOHNNY: They're like the same age.

CLAUDIA: Huh. Okay, good. I hope you get it. Janitor at the temple. Just—let me get some work done. I get paid by the click. I'll go down the list real fast and do some comments—

JOHNNY: Sounds like a fun job.

(Claudia sits at the computer.)

CLAUDIA: It's okay. Go play Cave War. We'll have sex and pizza when I'm done.

(Claudia works. She clicks mostly. Sometimes she writes a comment. Johnny is antsy. He goes to a shelf of books and searches for something to read.)

CLAUDIA: *(At the computer screen.)* It's awesome!

JOHNNY: What is?

CLAUDIA: Just this hair gel stuff.

JOHNNY: Oh.

(Claudia continues to work while Johnny looks at the shelf of books.)

JOHNNY: You ever read the Bible?

CLAUDIA: No.

(Johnny takes the Bible off the shelf and sits on the couch and reads.)

CLAUDIA: Like!

JOHNNY: It's kind of cool. The stories. The Torah is the first five books of the Bible.

CLAUDIA: Like!

(Johnny reads.)

JOHNNY: The rabbi told me that The Chosen Ones has nothing to do with being superior.

CLAUDIA: *(To the computer.)* Best Dog Food Ever!

JOHNNY: God chose Abraham and his people to spread the word of One God or something.

CLAUDIA: My dog can't get enough! And his coat is so shiny.

(Johnny continues to read. Claudia keeps clicking.)

CLAUDIA: Love it!

JOHNNY: The Land of Canaan is real. It's in the Middle East, which is cool. The Holy Land.

CLAUDIA: Why are you reading that?

JOHNNY: I'm Jewish.

CLAUDIA: You weren't raised—your mother doesn't do that.

JOHNNY: I know. But my father, he was definitely Jewish.

CLAUDIA: You didn't know him, Johnny.

JOHNNY: Yeah I did.

CLAUDIA: No you didn't.

JOHNNY: He's in me.

(Claudia gives Johnny a concerned look, turns, and clicks another LIKE.)

CLAUDIA: Like.

JOHNNY: Deuteronomy is a funny name.

CLAUDIA: Like.

(Claudia looks at Johnny.)

CLAUDIA: Why don't you play Cave War with that guy in Finland?

(Claudia goes back to work. Johnny reads the Bible.)

JOHNNY: *(Teasing, testing.)* In the beginning—

CLAUDIA: Johnny!

JOHNNY: —God created the heavens and the earth.

CLAUDIA: Let me work.

(Claudia continues to LIKE things online.)

CLAUDIA: Cool.

(Johnny continues to read.)

JOHNNY: Huh.

CLAUDIA: Wow, that's ugly ... Like!

JOHNNY: Leviticus. You heard of him?

CLAUDIA: The pink one.

JOHNNY: Huh.

CLAUDIA: Leave me alone.

JOHNNY: Aren't you curious?

CLAUDIA: Everything's working out. You don't need to read that.

(Johnny gets up with his Bible and kind of rubs Claudia's back with it to tease and annoy.)

JOHNNY: It was the rabbi's idea. To dive into it. He has some good ideas. We talked a lot. He's a nice guy.

CLAUDIA: I bet he is. But you don't need to read the Bible to mop floors.

JOHNNY: This is what you want, isn't it?

(Johnny jumps and bites Claudia in the middle of her back and holds on. It's different than usual. It hurts more than it should. Vengeful.)

CLAUDIA: Ow! ... No, Wait! ... Okay. Stop!

(Johnny stops.)

JOHNNY: I stopped.

CLAUDIA: Thank you. Jesus, Johnny.

JOHNNY: It's a little humiliating, right?

(Claudia's cell phone rings. She answers it.)

CLAUDIA: Uh-huh ... Yeah ... Okay ... Yeah ...

(Something is wrong. Johnny rubs Claudia's hair, nice.)

CLAUDIA: We'll talk tomorrow … It's okay. Thanks, Sonia.

(Claudia hangs up.)

JOHNNY: What's going on?

CLAUDIA: My mother's dead.

JOHNNY: Wow.

(Claudia sighs.)

JOHNNY: Is there going to be a funeral?

CLAUDIA: I don't think so.

JOHNNY: Claudia, I'm sorry.

(Johnny hugs her.)

JOHNNY: You okay?

CLAUDIA: I don't know.

(Johnny picks up a can of tomatoes.)

JOHNNY: I'll make us some dinner.

CLAUDIA: I never knew her.

(Johnny lovingly looks at Claudia and gives her a little sweet kiss.)

CLAUDIA: Thank you.

(Claudia shuts her computer. She looks around the room.)

JOHNNY: You okay?

CLAUDIA: I thought I would feel different.

Scene 10

(Sonia stands alone in the middle of the apartment with two large suitcases. Claudia speaks from the kitchen.)

SONIA: Where do you want your stuff?

CLAUDIA: Uh—Just leave them there. Thanks for hauling them over. I could have gotten them tomorrow.

SONIA: Carlos gave me a ride. So … Is there anything I can do?

CLAUDIA: Johnny'll be right back with the ice.

SONIA: Okay.

(Sonia looks around at the place. She wheels the two suitcases to the side and then stacks one on top of the other against the wall. The cart of water still sits in the middle of the living room. Sonia wheels it back and forth and stands there holding onto the cart. Claudia enters with a small free paper calendar from a dry cleaner store.)

CLAUDIA: So which weekend in August is the better one?

SONIA: It's gotten more complicated.

CLAUDIA: With Carlos? Where is he?

SONIA: I'm going to North Carolina.

CLAUDIA: Yeah?

SONIA: I got the job at the fishing magazine. I'm going to go. In a few days.

CLAUDIA: Okay. Wow, Sonia, great. You'll fly back for the wedding?

(Noise in the hallway. Sydelle reprimands Johnny.)

SYDELLE: No one cares who Bathsheba is!

(Johnny enters with bags of ice. Sydelle follows him.)

JOHNNY: You should!

SYDELLE: Stay away from the internet. You're getting yourself all worked up.

SONIA: Hi Johnny.

JOHNNY: Hi.

SONIA: What can I do? Should I open these waters?

CLAUDIA: No, no, they're for Brian.

JOHNNY: Have a seat, Mom.

SYDELLE: Okay.

(The buzzer buzzes. Claudia hits the button.)

SYDELLE: So let's pick a date.

CLAUDIA: We're still talking about the end of August. Sonia can come back from North Carolina.

JOHNNY: You're really going?

SONIA: Yeah. And sooner than I thought.

SYDELLE: You have to get rid of this water.

CLAUDIA: *(To Sydelle.)* Sonia got the job with the fishing magazine.

SYDELLE: *(To Sonia.)* Congratulations. I didn't know you were a fishing expert.

SONIA: I don't know anything about fish. But it's a good job.

SYDELLE: Oh. *(To Claudia.)* I'm sorry about your mother.

CLAUDIA: It's okay.

SYDELLE: You should have called me.

CLAUDIA: Eh—

SYDELLE: But it was your mother.

CLAUDIA: She wasn't my mother!

SONIA: She was your mother, Claudia.

CLAUDIA: She was an old drug addict who pushed me out of her body back before she pickled it up and burned it out.

SYDELLE: Jesus.

SONIA: Kind of true—

(A knock at the door. Claudia answers it. Brian comes in. He has a bottle of wine. It's getting physically tight and awkward.)

CLAUDIA: Hi Brian. This is Brian.

BRIAN: Hello.

CLAUDIA: This is Sonia and Sydelle.

BRIAN: Hello.

SYDELLE: Hello, Brian.

SONIA: Hi.

BRIAN: *(Handing the wine over.)* This is for you.

CLAUDIA: Thank you. I'll open it. Johnny, where's the wine opener?

JOHNNY: Do we have one?

CLAUDIA: I thought—I think we do.

BRIAN: We can have it later.

SYDELLE: It's in the drawer with all the spatulas next to the stove.

JOHNNY: I have some ice.

SYDELLE: What's the ice for?

CLAUDIA: To keep the beer cold.

SONIA: This water—

BRIAN: I can move the water over here.

JOHNNY: I got it.

(Johnny moves the water. He grabs the ice and goes into the bathroom. Sound of ice filling a tub.)

CLAUDIA: Dinner's almost ready. I figured everyone would be hungry so we can just eat right away.

BRIAN: Sounds good.

(Johnny comes out, grabs the beer and brings it back to the bathroom.)

SYDELLE: I could eat.

(Claudia pulls dinner together. She speaks from the kitchen.)

CLAUDIA: I found the wine opener!

SONIA: Where are you from, Brian?

BRIAN: About a half hour from here.

SYDELLE: I live a few blocks away.

(Sound of beer going into the ice in the bathroom.)

SONIA: I live over that way but I'm moving to North Carolina.

BRIAN: I've never been there.

(Johnny comes back in with five beers and pops them open.)

JOHNNY: They're still a little cold from the store.

BRIAN: Thanks.

SONIA: Thank you.

SYDELLE: Thank you, Johnny.

(Quiet as they all drink. Claudia is clambering around the food.)

CLAUDIA: Almost ready!

JOHNNY: I'll get the veggies.

(Johnny joins Claudia.)

BRIAN: *(To Sonia.)* Why North Carolina?

SONIA: I got a job.

SYDELLE: A fishing magazine.

BRIAN: I don't know anything about fishing.

SYDELLE: She doesn't either. But who does?

SONIA: *(To Brian.)* Where do you work?

CLAUDIA: Coming in!

(Claudia enters with a big cookie sheet of pizza buns. Johnny enters with a bowl of celery and carrots and blue cheese dressing. They are put on a table. Paper plates and napkins, too.)

BRIAN: They smell great.

CLAUDIA: No one ever doesn't like them.

SYDELLE: I'll serve.

SONIA: That's okay. I have it.

JOHNNY: Everyone just help yourselves.

SONIA: You sure?

CLAUDIA: Yeah. Just grab them. *(Brandishing the wine opener.)* Whenever anyone's ready for the wine Brian brought. *(To Brian.)* Thank you.

BRIAN: We can have it after the beer and buns.

(Sydelle has to move the cart of water to get to the pizza buns. Claudia puts the wine opener in her back pocket.)

SONIA: What IS all this water?

CLAUDIA: It's a gift for Brian.

JOHNNY: The water where he lives is kind of weird.

CLAUDIA: For everyone there. That whole part of town. They test it and sometimes it's not right.

BRIAN: Bad pipes.

SONIA: In Charlotte everything is pretty new. I mean, it's all glass and steel. I don't know.

SYDELLE: What's Carlos going to do down there?

(Everyone has their pizza buns.)

SONIA: He's not going. We broke up.

CLAUDIA: What?

SONIA: The day your mother died.

BRIAN: Your mother died?

SONIA: That's why I didn't tell you. I just have to get away from him, from everything. I'm choking.

(Johnny rolls the water to another spot.)

CLAUDIA: Leave it, Johnny.

JOHNNY: It's in the way.

SONIA: Someone always trying to tell me what to do. At home. At work. What to think. How to act. Things have to be better in Charlotte.

BRIAN: It's an animal thing. Dominance. The pecking order, really.

CLAUDIA: *(Liking what Brian said.)* Like chickens?

BRIAN: Yeah. We're not that different from other animals, really.

CLAUDIA: I love animals.

(Johnny notices Claudia noticing Brian.)

SONIA: Maybe I'll get a dog.

SYDELLE: Don't do it.

(Johnny struggles with the cart of water.)

CLAUDIA: *(To Johnny.)* Just leave it.

JOHNNY: It's really in the way. Hold on.

(Johnny tries to roll the water out of the apartment.)

CLAUDIA: It's fine.

(Claudia stops Johnny.)

JOHNNY: Anyone need another beer?

SONIA/BRIAN/SYDELLE: I'm good./No thanks./Not yet.

CLAUDIA: So, we're talking about a date in August. Sonia can come back for it.

BRIAN: Great! Here's to the couple.

(Everyone clinks bottles.)

CLAUDIA: The last Friday good for everyone? Make sense?

SONIA/BRIAN: Sure./Sure.

SYDELLE: I have no other plans.

CLAUDIA: *(To Sonia.)* It's definitely over with you and Carlos?

SONIA: Oh yes.

SYDELLE: Why'd you break up?

SONIA: It was the horns.

SYDELLE: Was he a goat?

SONIA: He'd put on the music with all those horns. He wanted me to like it, but I hated it. And no matter how much I'd beg him to shut it off he wouldn't.

SYDELLE: He was just selfish then.

BRIAN: They say the kind of music you like is the music you listened to when you were twelve. That's when your brain really locks it in.

JOHNNY: *(Skeptically.)* Who says that?

BRIAN: It was an article. I read stuff like that.

CLAUDIA: *(Liking.)* He does.

SONIA: One night, two weeks ago, we were getting romantic and I said—Carlos, I can't do this with that shit playing. It's like I'm being attacked. I hate it—

BRIAN: That's pretty insulting.

SONIA: Oh he's a Buddhist. And I don't want to stereotype, I don't, but they're all passive aggressive. Like, they pretend they are on this journey of enlightenment but really, it's all about pleasuring themselves. It's masturbation.

SYDELLE: Only if they do it right, I guess?

SONIA: And if you don't act like a perfect little Buddhist—and on top of that like his annoying music—and then do everything else he tells you to do—

BRIAN: If you look at it with detachment, like a Buddhist, and scientifically, like a Westerner, there's a math to it. Cause and effect. He probably has a fear of you not being like him. These buns are great—

JOHNNY: *(Not liking Brian.)* Yeah, everyone likes science.

CLAUDIA: We watch animal videos.

SONIA: I just hate Buddhists.

BRIAN: How can you hate Buddhists? Everyone loves Buddhists.

SONIA: One of the reasons I'm moving to Charlotte is that there are almost no Buddhists there.

SYDELLE: There are almost no Buddhists, here.

SONIA: There's enough of them.

BRIAN: They say meditation can put many years on your life. They accept all faiths. It's good for everyone.

JOHNNY: Jewish people?

SYDELLE: Oh my God. Don't start, John—

CLAUDIA: Does anyone want more pizza buns?

SONIA: I'll have ten more.

CLAUDIA: And take some vegetables.

SONIA: I like Jewish people a hell of a lot more than Buddhists. My experience has been—and I don't want to stereotype—but Jewish people seem to be very honest and direct. Buddhists lie right to your face.

(Johnny goes to the bookshelf and gets the Bible.)

CLAUDIA: I didn't know Carlos was such a Buddhist. I just thought he liked to wear pajamas.

BRIAN: *(Trying to change the subject, to Claudia.)* Are you having anyone officiate at the wedding?

JOHNNY: The rabbi, maybe.

CLAUDIA: *(To Brian, really saying No.)* I don't know.

JOHNNY: Listen to this.

CLAUDIA: What are you doing, Johnny?

JOHNNY: Looking for the section. The first five books of the Bible is the Torah. Here. Numbers, 23:24.

SYDELLE: John, put that garbage away. You should quit that janitor job.

BRIAN: You got a job?

JOHNNY: I'm working at the temple.

BRIAN: You can probably get married there.

CLAUDIA: We'll just get married downtown. We'll all have a nice dinner. Family style.

SYDELLE: Five or six people?

JOHNNY: Listen. *(Reading.)* "No misfortune is seen in Jacob, no misery observed in Israel. The Lord their God is with them; the shout of the King is among them."

SYDELLE: John, you have guests. No one needs to hear this right now.

JOHNNY: Hold on. *(Reading.)* "God brought them out of Egypt; they have the strength of a wild ox. There is no divination against Jacob, no evil omens against Israel."

SONIA: I've gotta go. I'm in an awful mood.

CLAUDIA: Johnny!

SYDELLE: Give me that.

JOHNNY: *(Reading.)* "It will now be said of Jacob and of Israel, 'See what God has done!'"

BRIAN: Then what?

JOHNNY: *(Reading.)* "The people rise like a lioness; they rouse themselves like a lion that does not rest till it devours its prey and drinks the blood of its victims." Isn't that cool?

CLAUDIA: They talk about lions eating zebras in that thing?

(Sydelle approaches Johnny and grabs the Bible from him.)

SYDELLE: What are you doing?

JOHNNY: This is hardcore! It's interesting.

SYDELLE: To who?

JOHNNY: These people. These are some words, from God, or maybe not from God, I don't know, but some words about some really kickass people. They survive through everything. They're amazing.

SYDELLE: It's just a story. Let's put it away.

(Sydelle walks across the room and she looks at the books.)

JOHNNY: *(To Claudia.)* We should be like lions!

CLAUDIA: We ARE Johnny!

SYDELLE: You see this?

(Sydelle takes a book off an upper shelf.)

JOHNNY: What is it?

SYDELLE: It's a book on Norse mythology. Right next to the one about Greek mythology.

CLAUDIA: *(To Sonia, near door.)* Just wait, Sonia.

JOHNNY: So?

SYDELLE: When you were a kid, you were obsessed with mythology. Odin and Loki—all that otherworld stuff. It's a story, John. A fantasy like your computer game, Cave Wars.

(Sydelle puts the Norse mythology book back.)

JOHNNY: The Bible isn't just stories.

SYDELLE: Yeah it is. I'm taking this Bible and I'm putting it on the shelf right next to the mythologies. Where it belongs.

(Sydelle slams the Bible up on the shelf.)

SONIA: Jesus.

CLAUDIA: Sonia—

SONIA: I have to go. I'm sorry. Claudia—

CLAUDIA: End of August then.

SONIA: Yeah, end of August. Last Friday. I'll fly back. Bring a fish.

(Sonia leaves.)

SYDELLE: You can't—we are not religious people.

JOHNNY: People convert. I want to be a part—

(Claudia is flushed.)

SYDELLE: Claudia?

CLAUDIA: *(Hating this.)* Yeah?

SYDELLE: *(To Johnny.)* You see her face? She's not

into this. You two are getting married, fine! Be practical! Why are you doing this to yourself?

JOHNNY: *(To Sydelle.)* WHY ARE YOU SO AGAINST BEING JEWISH!?

SYDELLE: My parents assimilated. I assimilated. That's not even the—I'm just an American person.

JOHNNY: If my father were here, he'd have something to say about that.

SYDELLE: Your father didn't talk much. This is all about your father?

JOHNNY: I want to see my father. I want to see one picture of my father. How could you not have even one picture of him?

CLAUDIA: Johnny—

JOHNNY: *(To Claudia.)* Maybe you don't care about your dead mother. But I care about my dead father.

SYDELLE: Johnny! You want to know what happened to the pictures of your father? Really?

JOHNNY: Yeah.

SYDELLE: He wasn't special. Your father was what they used to call a scoundrel. A womanizer. He left us. Not long after, he died of a heart attack. You were young. It all ended. It had nothing to do with you and I hated him. There it is. I'm sorry. But that's that.

JOHNNY: And not one picture?

SYDELLE: After he took off, I gathered up all the pictures. I went down to the street to the trash cans and lucky for me a huge garbage truck was right in front of the building.

JOHNNY: No—

SYDELLE: And you know how that big part at the back compacts all the garbage? It was just starting to come down—and I threw all the pictures into the stinky mess of rotten food. I watched the truck smash everything into the wet liquid garbage. That's where the photos went. It was my lucky day.

CLAUDIA: Wow.

SYDELLE: What a great man of God he was. He was nothing. He didn't love me. He barely knew you. And every trace of him has long been rotting in some dump. Did he go to temple? Sure. Sometimes. To pick up women. And he died and left us with nothing. What a stupid story. So unique. I can't even believe I had to tell it to you. Write this on the last page of your Torah— "And the Jews were left with NOTHING!"

(Pause.)

SYDELLE: So now you know. It's the oldest story of them all. Father leaves family. Then the kids idolize him. He can go to hell.

CLAUDIA: I'm sorry, Johnny. I kind of had a feeling—

JOHNNY: Fine. We done? We pick a date?

SYDELLE: Last Friday in August.

(Pause.)

SYDELLE: I have an early shift tomorrow.

BRIAN: *(To Sydelle.)* I'll walk you home.

SYDELLE *(To Brian.)* Thank you. *(Close, to Johnny.)* Quit that job. I'll call some of my lady friends at the library and get you some work. You can clean the toilets there if you like to read so much. Johnny, I'm sorry about your father. But please—

(Brian and Sydelle leave. Johnny and Claudia are alone. Johnny stares at the cart.)

JOHNNY: He left the cart here.

CLAUDIA: He's walking your mother home. We'll—I'll get it to him. That was a good dinner. You want another bun?

JOHNNY: Claudia?

CLAUDIA: I'm sorry about your dad. But, Johnny—

JOHNNY: Claudia?

CLAUDIA: We have a date. We have witnesses. A nice group, don't you think? It's going to be a great day. When we get old and our kids are grown we can tell them how we got married and how we lived in this little apartment your mother had since you were in the third grade. How we played around—

(Claudia jumps on Johnny to bite him. He holds her off.)

JOHNNY: Stop.

CLAUDIA: Come on.

JOHNNY: It's annoying. I told you, I don't like it.

CLAUDIA: I'm sorry about your father, Johnny. Sounds like he was a bad guy. I had a feeling. He was like my mom. Not the marrying type.

JOHNNY: Brian seems like the marrying type.

CLAUDIA: I think so, too!

JOHNNY: Why don't you marry him?

CLAUDIA: Be nice—

JOHNNY: He's a scientist. You guys can make robots together.

CLAUDIA: Stop it. We're getting married, Johnny. Help me clean up.

JOHNNY: You hang on his every word. You did it at lunch and then tonight you talked about chickens.

CLAUDIA: He's our friend!

JOHNNY: Yeah?

CLAUDIA: When did we talk about chickens? …

(Claudia holds him by his two arms and looks at him in the eyes.)

JOHNNY: … Stay at Sonia's tonight.

CLAUDIA: Don't make me bite you.

JOHNNY: Yeah, that's not going to happen.

CLAUDIA: I can be Jewish, Johnny, if that's what you want. But I don't want to read the Bible. It sounds crazy. The Jewish people are like a really big tribe, right? Let's do it. August. I'm sorry about your dad. I understand. We'll be Jewish. And if we don't like that, we can try something else.

JOHNNY: Claudia?

CLAUDIA: I said I'll do it, if that's what you want. For you and your father.

JOHNNY: You don't know my father.

CLAUDIA: I feel him, too, Johnny.

JOHNNY: No you don't. Stay with Sonia 'til she moves to North Carolina. I want to get some reading done.

CLAUDIA: So you can become some religious person? Without me?

JOHNNY: So I can do what I want!

CLAUDIA: She's leaving in a few days. I have an idea—

(Johnny goes to the bookshelf and takes down the Bible.)

JOHNNY: I have to work in the morning. Go to Sonia's.

CLAUDIA: Sure. Okay, Johnny. You're upset. One minute.

JOHNNY: You love Brian.

CLAUDIA: That's crazy—

JOHNNY: You do.

CLAUDIA: How could I? He's not Jewish!

(Claudia goes to the kitchen. Johnny stares at the cart of water. Claudia returns with a sharp paring knife. She puts it on the table.)

CLAUDIA: Sit.

JOHNNY: What for?

CLAUDIA: Take off your pants.

JOHNNY: Why?

CLAUDIA: I'm going to help you. Take your pants off. I have a surprise for you.

(Johnny sits but does not take off his pants.)

CLAUDIA: You don't have a father, Johnny. I understand. You want to be part of his tradition. There's like, something we need to fix here.

(Claudia points the paring knife at Johnny.)

JOHNNY: What the hell are you doing?

CLAUDIA: You're really only missing one thing. We'll take care of that. It'll be fun.

JOHNNY: Go home.

CLAUDIA: You just need to be circumcised. Relax.

JOHNNY: Yeah, Claudia. Great idea. Go.

CLAUDIA: We've watched this a hundred times. We like stuff like this. This is us.

JOHNNY: You really think that knife is coming anywhere near my dick? Go to Sonia's.

CLAUDIA: If you were a baby—

JOHNNY: You're not circumcising me. You're insane. Go.

(Claudia jumps on Johnny's lap.)

85

CLAUDIA: Listen. I'm not going to hurt you. Maasai boys used to have to kill a lion in order to become a man.

JOHNNY: Get off me.

CLAUDIA: But they're modern now, so they only have to pretend to kill one, in their mind. It's a ritual.

JOHNNY: Get off me with that knife Claudia.

CLAUDIA: Pretend to be circumcised. Pretend it.

JOHNNY: If I want to get circumcised I'll get it done for real.

CLAUDIA: Close your eyes. Like the boys in Africa pretend to kill the lion, you pretend you're getting circumcised.

JOHNNY: This is stupid, Claudia.

CLAUDIA: Just pretend.

JOHNNY: Put the knife down.

(Claudia puts the knife down.)

JOHNNY: Get off me.

(Claudia gets off him.)

CLAUDIA: Close your eyes. Close your eyes and pretend, Johnny. If that's what you want—Pretend you're Jewish. Then you'll feel part of your history. This will be fun. And then we can get married. Anywhere you like.

JOHNNY: I'm sorry, Claudia. But enough—

CLAUDIA: That's okay. We'll be Jewish. I'm fine. I'm here to help you.

JOHNNY: This isn't helping.

(Johnny picks up the knife and throws it across the room.)

CLAUDIA: You have a good imagination. You can do this. It'll be fast. Close your eyes.

JOHNNY: I don't want to. Enough, Claudia.

CLAUDIA: This will just take two seconds. Just two seconds!

JOHNNY: Sure. Then you'll go to Sonia's?

CLAUDIA: Whatever you like. This is your special day.

JOHNNY: Fine.

(Johnny closes his eyes.)

CLAUDIA: Good. Think of us. Think of our future. And the future of our children. You're getting circumcised right now. And it's easy. It's going without a hitch. And you can be a part of your history. And then we'll get married.

JOHNNY: Sure—

CLAUDIA: It's okay. Keep your eyes closed.

JOHNNY: Claudia—

CLAUDIA: Just imagine—someone's cutting you. Like the African boys, use your imagination.

JOHNNY: Fine.

CLAUDIA: You see the guy—the doctor or the rabbi or—

JOHNNY: It's going to have to be a doctor—I'm too old for a mohel.

CLAUDIA: So you're at the doctor's office and it's sort of a holy place. And you're numb and he's cutting you.

JOHNNY: Okay, Claudia.

CLAUDIA: Getting rid of that skin you don't need.

JOHNNY: I can see it.

(Claudia takes the wine opener out from her pocket. Opens the knife end.)

CLAUDIA: Good, right? Almost done now. Fast and easy. Stand up. Keep your eyes closed. Lower your pants. Just a little.

JOHNNY: No, Claudia.

CLAUDIA: I'll do it.

(Claudia lowers Johnny's pants a little. He lets her without a struggle.)

CLAUDIA: Let's finish up then.

(Johnny opens his eyes. Claudia grabs him by the thigh and slices down.)

JOHNNY: Ow! What's wrong with you?

(There is blood. Johnny runs from her and flattens against a wall. He looks inside his underwear. Johnny is transfixed by the blood.)

CLAUDIA: You're a man now. A drop of blood makes it a little more real, right? Show us.

JOHNNY: Claudia?

CLAUDIA: Yeah?

(Long pause.)

JOHNNY: I need you to go.

CLAUDIA: Let's clean up.

JOHNNY: We're not getting married, Claudia.

CLAUDIA: I'll go with you to the temple on fourteenth, Johnny. I won't believe in God or anything, but I can just be like the people who go to church and then do whatever they like, I could be like them. Right? We can do that.

JOHNNY: You'll never be Jewish, Claudia.

CLAUDIA: Whatever you want, Johnny. When do we start?

JOHNNY: You have to go. You have to go for good.

CLAUDIA: We have to clean up. I just nicked your leg. I'll get you a Band-Aid.

JOHNNY: I don't need one.

(Johnny puts a napkin on the cut.)

CLAUDIA: You sure?

(Claudia rinses the sharp end of the wine opener with beer.)

CLAUDIA: Now it's my turn. You want to cut me? I don't need to pretend some ritual. Just do it.

JOHNNY: No.

(Claudia lowers her pants to show her legs.)

CLAUDIA: Go ahead. Then we'll both be initiated. We'll be like lions, Johnny. Like in the Bible.

(Johnny closes the wine opener. He takes a real long look at Claudia.)

JOHNNY: I want you to leave.

CLAUDIA: Come on! Give me a cut. Something superficial!

JOHNNY: We rise up like lions. We don't take them down.

CLAUDIA: The Maasai do.

JOHNNY: We are not Maasai. Go with Sonia to North Carolina.

CLAUDIA: I'm not going to North Carolina. Sonia doesn't want me to go. Can't you tell? Come on, my turn.

JOHNNY: Then go talk to Brian. He's so smart, he'll tell you what you can do.

(Claudia picks up the wine opener. She opens it. To cut herself or Johnny, it is unclear. Johnny jumps on top of Claudia and pins her to the sofa.)

JOHNNY: Listen to me. You leave here and never come back. You don't know me. You don't love me. You go.

CLAUDIA: Stop it!

JOHNNY: I'm not doing this anymore.

CLAUDIA: Get off of me!

JOHNNY: Look at me … I never want to see you again. You understand?

CLAUDIA: Yeah, Johnny, sure.

JOHNNY: Don't ever touch me again. Don't ever call me again. Nothing.

CLAUDIA: Okay, Johnny, just get offa me.

(Johnny gets up. Claudia gets up.)

CLAUDIA: I'll go to Sonia's tonight. You calm down. I'll see you tomorrow. We'll talk about getting married at the temple if it's so important. But it's just going to be easier downtown.

(Johnny wheels Claudia's suitcases and the cart of water into the hall.)

CLAUDIA: I can't carry all that. Leave those in here.

JOHNNY: Give me your keys.

CLAUDIA: No, Johnny.

JOHNNY: Give me your keys!

CLAUDIA: I'm sorry about your father, Johnny. He was a bad guy. You don't have to be a bad guy, too.

JOHNNY: I'm not a bad guy. Give me your keys.

CLAUDIA: No, Johnny.

JOHNNY: I'll change the locks, then.

CLAUDIA: Right. Do that. You change the locks.

JOHNNY: You understand what I'm doing here?

CLAUDIA: See you tomorrow, Johnny.

(Claudia walks out, past the suitcases and the water. She'll be back tomorrow.)

Scene 11

(Park outside Claudia's old job. Claudia sits with her two suitcases and the cart of bottled water. It is evening. A beautiful purple sky. She is on her cell phone leaving a message.)

CLAUDIA: Johnny, I left my charger at your place and I'm running out of juice. I think I have to cancel my phone anyway. But hold onto the charger for me. In case. Good luck ... with everything.

(Claudia hangs up the phone. She unzips a suitcase and takes out a can of tomatoes. She smashes her cell phone to smithereens. She opens one of the flats of water and takes out a bottle, opens it and sips. She looks out at the sky. She checks to make sure no one will get hurt. Then she throws the dented can of tomatoes as hard as she can. Brian shows up.)

CLAUDIA: You forgot your water.

BRIAN: I really can't take it.

CLAUDIA: Why not?

BRIAN: The elevator in my building doesn't work. I'm on the twelfth floor. I should have said something. So—it's just—I'm sorry.

CLAUDIA: Okay.

BRIAN: My job isn't in this building anymore. They moved.

CLAUDIA: I'm glad you still have your job.

BRIAN: Where are you going to go?

CLAUDIA: I don't know.

BRIAN: What about Sonia?

CLAUDIA: She's gone. I wasn't invited.

(Brian looks at the ground at the smashed phone.)

BRIAN: Is that yours?

CLAUDIA: Yeah.

(Brian kicks at it with his foot to get it away from her.)

BRIAN: These things are toxic inside.

CLAUDIA: Kids from Asia, right?

(Brian continues to kick at the pieces. Claudia stares out.)

CLAUDIA: I wanted to marry Johnny. I loved him. We could have made our own little tribe. With friends like you. Like normal people in a little town in Canada or Africa. A place where you always know there is someone there.

BRIAN: Like a club or a church?

CLAUDIA: A simple office job or be on a team—

BRIAN: High finance or a street gang. Doctors without Borders.

CLAUDIA: Just a little village. Something simple. Just, like, be a person.

BRIAN: Yeah, people can be anything. It's plasticity.

CLAUDIA: What's that?

BRIAN: The brain changes according to experience. So people can become anything really.

CLAUDIA: That's a nice idea.

BRIAN: But the underlying structure, the basic setup is there. It's how the wiring is built. But the needs of each brain are different. So everyone can do it their own way.

CLAUDIA: So people can be anything.

BRIAN: Yeah.

CLAUDIA: Johnny thinks I love you.

BRIAN: I thought he was a good guy, at first. You wanted my opinion of Johnny. But Claudia—

CLAUDIA: It doesn't matter now. I bet he ends up in a cult or something. He changed the locks. Three days ago.

BRIAN: I didn't know it was three days—

CLAUDIA: Well, four, really, if you count the front door of the building.

(Brian looks at Claudia's luggage.)

CLAUDIA: Brian?

(Brian puts his hand on Claudia's shoulder. Claudia takes his arm and tries to bite his wrist, nice.)

BRIAN: What are you doing?

CLAUDIA: Just kidding around.

BRIAN: I don't like to be bitten.

CLAUDIA: Okay … Brian?

BRIAN: I don't love you, Claudia.

CLAUDIA: I didn't think so. That's okay. We don't know each other very well.

BRIAN: I'm sorry you don't have someone Claudia. A father, a mother. If I had a breast, I'd take it out and I would put it in your mouth. If I raised you, I'd teach you to be proud of yourself and to not take any guff from anyone. Teach you how to stop biting. So things would get better. To know yourself.

CLAUDIA: Me and Johnny—we didn't know each other.

BRIAN: Maybe not enough …

CLAUDIA: … I don't care about religion or games or the Bible or any of that stuff.

BRIAN: Me either, other than as an interesting study.

CLAUDIA: Johnny thinks I love you. But it was an excuse. He just—he couldn't do it.

BRIAN: Sorry. The way it ended. Sorry.

CLAUDIA: I just need new context. You know?

BRIAN: Sure. I only have a few minutes, between classes—So—

CLAUDIA: Brian? Can I meet your mother?

BRIAN: Why?

CLAUDIA: I need a job.

BRIAN: She doesn't hire people.

CLAUDIA: Maybe she can teach me how to do medical stuff. I'm good at filling things out on the computer.

BRIAN: They always need that. But—

CLAUDIA: *(Has never needed anything more than this.)* So maybe you can introduce me? To your mom? Please? I really want to meet your mother.

BRIAN: I don't know, Claudia. What happened to your job?

CLAUDIA: I don't think I liked things enough ... Please?

BRIAN: Sure. I'll introduce you to my mother.

CLAUDIA: Can we go right now?

BRIAN: After my class is over we can go.

(They each take a suitcase. Claudia tries to push the water, too.)

BRIAN: Leave that there. Someone else might need it.

CLAUDIA: Okay.

(Claudia takes out three bottles. She puts two in her suitcase and hands one to Brian.)

BRIAN: Thank you.

CLAUDIA: We could do something that's never been done before, Brian. We could start our own tribe, based on nothing. On water. That's all we need. We'll be the water tribe.

BRIAN: Nothing more basic than that.

CLAUDIA: Thank you, Brian ... I tried with Johnny. I even circumcised him.

BRIAN: Really?

CLAUDIA: Just pretend.

(Pause. Brian takes this in. He tries to hide his recoil.)

BRIAN: I really have to fly. I'm late. Why don't you just wait here—

CLAUDIA: I'll just wait outside your—where is it?

BRIAN: I'll come back after my class is over. This is a better place to wait. Okay?

CLAUDIA: Okay. I'll see you after your class ... Brian?

BRIAN: Yeah?

CLAUDIA: It's what Johnny wanted. It really was pretend. I hope they take him now. He's lonely.

(Brian walks off. Claudia sits with the two suitcases and the cart of water. She knows Brian may not come back but she waits.)

The End

NOTES

Made in the USA
Columbia, SC
16 February 2023